BULL

$$$ $$$

TO THE MOON

Stock Trading And Investing Journal

© Copyright 2021 - Sleek Press Publishing
All Rights Reserved

```
┌ ─ ─ ─ ─ ─ ─ ─ ─ ─ ─ ─ ─ ─ ─ ─ ─ ─ ┐
│  THIS JOURNAL BELONGS TO:          │
│                                    │
│   _____          │
│   (GENIUS INVESTOR)                │
└ ─ ─ ─ ─ ─ ─ ─ ─ ─ ─ ─ ─ ─ ─ ─ ─ ─ ┘
```

"To The Moon and Beyond!"

— B.M. Genius

HOW TO USE THIS JOURNAL

This journal is intended to be used by the casual stock market investor. It's your everyday logbook for stocks you've recently traded or stumbled on. The stock entry pages allow you to record general details about the stock or company you are interested in – like the current price, market cap and P/E ratio. There's a simple trade log section for any Buy or Sell action on the stock. You can also write down reason(s) why you are interested in the stock or company in the 'Why I Like This Stock' section. Each stock entry page has a corresponding dotted journal entry page for you to write down your genius bull market thoughts and ideas.

Use the page tracker on the next page to record the stock symbol or company name and it's corresponding page number each time you add a new entry into your journal.

Page	STOCK	Page	STOCK

STOCK

Company name:

Ticker Symbol:

Industry:

Market Cap: P/E Ratio:

Current Price: Date:

Type:

☐ Value   ☐ Growth   ☐ Dividends

Short-term Outlook:

☐ Bearish   ☐ Neutral   ☐ Bullish

Mid-term Outlook:

☐ Bearish   ☐ Neutral   ☐ Bullish

Long-term Outlook:

☐ Bearish   ☐ Neutral   ☐ Bullish

TRADE LOG

☐ Bought [Date:_____]	☐ Sold [Date:_____]
Price:	Price:
Quantity:	Quantity:

WHY I LIKE THIS STOCK...

Genius Notes:

STOCK

Company name:

Ticker Symbol:

Industry:

Market Cap: P/E Ratio:

Current Price: Date:

Type:
    ☐ Value   ☐ Growth   ☐ Dividends

Short-term Outlook:
    ☐ Bearish   ☐ Neutral   ☐ Bullish

Mid-term Outlook:
    ☐ Bearish   ☐ Neutral   ☐ Bullish

Long-term Outlook:
    ☐ Bearish   ☐ Neutral   ☐ Bullish

TRADE LOG

☐ Bought [Date:_____]	☐ Sold [Date:_____]
Price:	Price:
Quantity:	Quantity:

WHY I LIKE THIS STOCK...

Genius Notes:

STOCK

Company name:

Ticker Symbol:

Industry:

Market Cap: P/E Ratio:

Current Price: Date:

Type:

☐ Value   ☐ Growth   ☐ Dividends

Short-term Outlook:

☐ Bearish   ☐ Neutral   ☐ Bullish

Mid-term Outlook:

☐ Bearish   ☐ Neutral   ☐ Bullish

Long-term Outlook:

☐ Bearish   ☐ Neutral   ☐ Bullish

TRADE LOG

☐ Bought [Date:_____]	☐ Sold [Date:_____]
Price:	Price:
Quantity:	Quantity:

WHY I LIKE THIS STOCK...

Genius Notes:

STOCK

Company name:

Ticker Symbol:

Industry:

Market Cap: P/E Ratio:

Current Price: Date:

Type:

☐ Value   ☐ Growth   ☐ Dividends

Short-term Outlook:

☐ Bearish   ☐ Neutral   ☐ Bullish

Mid-term Outlook:

☐ Bearish   ☐ Neutral   ☐ Bullish

Long-term Outlook:

☐ Bearish   ☐ Neutral   ☐ Bullish

TRADE LOG

☐ Bought [Date:_____]	☐ Sold [Date:_____]
Price:	Price:
Quantity:	Quantity:

WHY I LIKE THIS STOCK...

Genius Notes:

STOCK

Company name:

Ticker Symbol:

Industry:

Market Cap: P/E Ratio:

Current Price: Date:

Type:

☐ Value ☐ Growth ☐ Dividends

Short-term Outlook:

☐ Bearish ☐ Neutral ☐ Bullish

Mid-term Outlook:

☐ Bearish ☐ Neutral ☐ Bullish

Long-term Outlook:

☐ Bearish ☐ Neutral ☐ Bullish

TRADE LOG

☐ Bought [Date:_____]	☐ Sold [Date:_____]
Price:	Price:
Quantity:	Quantity:

WHY I LIKE THIS STOCK...

Genius Notes:

STOCK

Company name:

Ticker Symbol:

Industry:

Market Cap: P/E Ratio:

Current Price: Date:

Type:
    ☐ Value   ☐ Growth   ☐ Dividends

Short-term Outlook:
    ☐ Bearish   ☐ Neutral   ☐ Bullish

Mid-term Outlook:
    ☐ Bearish   ☐ Neutral   ☐ Bullish

Long-term Outlook:
    ☐ Bearish   ☐ Neutral   ☐ Bullish

TRADE LOG

☐ Bought [Date:_____]	☐ Sold [Date:_____]
Price:	Price:
Quantity:	Quantity:

WHY I LIKE THIS STOCK...

Genius Notes:

STOCK

Company name:

Ticker Symbol:

Industry:

Market Cap: P/E Ratio:

Current Price: Date:

Type:
    ☐ Value   ☐ Growth   ☐ Dividends

Short-term Outlook:
    ☐ Bearish   ☐ Neutral   ☐ Bullish

Mid-term Outlook:
    ☐ Bearish   ☐ Neutral   ☐ Bullish

Long-term Outlook:
    ☐ Bearish   ☐ Neutral   ☐ Bullish

TRADE LOG

☐ Bought [Date:_____]	☐ Sold [Date:_____]
Price:	Price:
Quantity:	Quantity:

WHY I LIKE THIS STOCK...

Genius Notes:

STOCK

Company name:

Ticker Symbol:

Industry:

Market Cap: P/E Ratio:

Current Price: Date:

Type:

    ☐ Value   ☐ Growth   ☐ Dividends

Short-term Outlook:

    ☐ Bearish   ☐ Neutral   ☐ Bullish

Mid-term Outlook:

    ☐ Bearish   ☐ Neutral   ☐ Bullish

Long-term Outlook:

    ☐ Bearish   ☐ Neutral   ☐ Bullish

TRADE LOG

☐ Bought [Date:_____]	☐ Sold [Date:_____]
Price:	Price:
Quantity:	Quantity:

WHY I LIKE THIS STOCK...

Genius Notes:

STOCK

Company name:

Ticker Symbol:

Industry:

Market Cap: P/E Ratio:

Current Price: Date:

Type:

☐ Value   ☐ Growth   ☐ Dividends

Short-term Outlook:

☐ Bearish   ☐ Neutral   ☐ Bullish

Mid-term Outlook:

☐ Bearish   ☐ Neutral   ☐ Bullish

Long-term Outlook:

☐ Bearish   ☐ Neutral   ☐ Bullish

TRADE LOG

☐ Bought [Date:_____]	☐ Sold [Date:_____]
Price:	Price:
Quantity:	Quantity:

WHY I LIKE THIS STOCK...

Genius Notes:

STOCK

Company name:

Ticker Symbol:

Industry:

Market Cap: P/E Ratio:

Current Price: Date:

Type:
- ☐ Value   ☐ Growth   ☐ Dividends

Short-term Outlook:
- ☐ Bearish   ☐ Neutral   ☐ Bullish

Mid-term Outlook:
- ☐ Bearish   ☐ Neutral   ☐ Bullish

Long-term Outlook:
- ☐ Bearish   ☐ Neutral   ☐ Bullish

TRADE LOG

☐ Bought [Date:_____]   ☐ Sold [Date:_____]

Price: Price:

Quantity: Quantity:

WHY I LIKE THIS STOCK...

Genius Notes:

STOCK

Company name:

Ticker Symbol:

Industry:

Market Cap: P/E Ratio:

Current Price: Date:

Type:
- ☐ Value   ☐ Growth   ☐ Dividends

Short-term Outlook:
- ☐ Bearish   ☐ Neutral   ☐ Bullish

Mid-term Outlook:
- ☐ Bearish   ☐ Neutral   ☐ Bullish

Long-term Outlook:
- ☐ Bearish   ☐ Neutral   ☐ Bullish

TRADE LOG

☐ Bought [Date:_____]	☐ Sold [Date:_____]
Price:	Price:
Quantity:	Quantity:

WHY I LIKE THIS STOCK...

Genius Notes:

STOCK

Company name:

Ticker Symbol:

Industry:

Market Cap: P/E Ratio:

Current Price: Date:

Type:

☐ Value   ☐ Growth   ☐ Dividends

Short-term Outlook:

☐ Bearish   ☐ Neutral   ☐ Bullish

Mid-term Outlook:

☐ Bearish   ☐ Neutral   ☐ Bullish

Long-term Outlook:

☐ Bearish   ☐ Neutral   ☐ Bullish

TRADE LOG

☐ Bought [Date:_____]	☐ Sold [Date:_____]
Price:	Price:
Quantity:	Quantity:

WHY I LIKE THIS STOCK...

Genius Notes:

STOCK

Company name:

Ticker Symbol:

Industry:

Market Cap: P/E Ratio:

Current Price: Date:

Type:
    ☐ Value   ☐ Growth   ☐ Dividends

Short-term Outlook:
    ☐ Bearish   ☐ Neutral   ☐ Bullish

Mid-term Outlook:
    ☐ Bearish   ☐ Neutral   ☐ Bullish

Long-term Outlook:
    ☐ Bearish   ☐ Neutral   ☐ Bullish

TRADE LOG

☐ Bought [Date:_____]	☐ Sold [Date:_____]
Price:	Price:
Quantity:	Quantity:

WHY I LIKE THIS STOCK...

Genius Notes:

STOCK

Company name:

Ticker Symbol:

Industry:

Market Cap: P/E Ratio:

Current Price: Date:

Type:

☐ Value   ☐ Growth   ☐ Dividends

Short-term Outlook:

☐ Bearish   ☐ Neutral   ☐ Bullish

Mid-term Outlook:

☐ Bearish   ☐ Neutral   ☐ Bullish

Long-term Outlook:

☐ Bearish   ☐ Neutral   ☐ Bullish

TRADE LOG

☐ Bought [Date:_____]	☐ Sold [Date:_____]
Price:	Price:
Quantity:	Quantity:

WHY I LIKE THIS STOCK...

Genius Notes:

STOCK

Company name:

Ticker Symbol:

Industry:

Market Cap: P/E Ratio:

Current Price: Date:

Type:

☐ Value ☐ Growth ☐ Dividends

Short-term Outlook:

☐ Bearish ☐ Neutral ☐ Bullish

Mid-term Outlook:

☐ Bearish ☐ Neutral ☐ Bullish

Long-term Outlook:

☐ Bearish ☐ Neutral ☐ Bullish

TRADE LOG

☐ Bought [Date:_____]	☐ Sold [Date:_____]
Price:	Price:
Quantity:	Quantity:

WHY I LIKE THIS STOCK...

Genius Notes:

STOCK

Company name:

Ticker Symbol:

Industry:

Market Cap: P/E Ratio:

Current Price: Date:

Type:

☐ Value   ☐ Growth   ☐ Dividends

Short-term Outlook:

☐ Bearish   ☐ Neutral   ☐ Bullish

Mid-term Outlook:

☐ Bearish   ☐ Neutral   ☐ Bullish

Long-term Outlook:

☐ Bearish   ☐ Neutral   ☐ Bullish

TRADE LOG

☐ Bought [Date:_____]	☐ Sold [Date:_____]
Price:	Price:
Quantity:	Quantity:

WHY I LIKE THIS STOCK...

Genius Notes:

STOCK

Company name:

Ticker Symbol:

Industry:

Market Cap: P/E Ratio:

Current Price: Date:

Type:

☐ Value   ☐ Growth   ☐ Dividends

Short-term Outlook:

☐ Bearish   ☐ Neutral   ☐ Bullish

Mid-term Outlook:

☐ Bearish   ☐ Neutral   ☐ Bullish

Long-term Outlook:

☐ Bearish   ☐ Neutral   ☐ Bullish

TRADE LOG

☐ Bought [Date:_____]   ☐ Sold [Date:_____]

Price: Price:

Quantity: Quantity:

WHY I LIKE THIS STOCK...

Genius Notes:

STOCK

Company name:

Ticker Symbol:

Industry:

Market Cap: P/E Ratio:

Current Price: Date:

Type:

☐ Value   ☐ Growth   ☐ Dividends

Short-term Outlook:

☐ Bearish   ☐ Neutral   ☐ Bullish

Mid-term Outlook:

☐ Bearish   ☐ Neutral   ☐ Bullish

Long-term Outlook:

☐ Bearish   ☐ Neutral   ☐ Bullish

TRADE LOG

☐ Bought [Date:_____]	☐ Sold [Date:_____]
Price:	Price:
Quantity:	Quantity:

WHY I LIKE THIS STOCK...

Genius Notes:

STOCK

Company name:

Ticker Symbol:

Industry:

Market Cap: P/E Ratio:

Current Price: Date:

Type:

   ☐ Value   ☐ Growth   ☐ Dividends

Short-term Outlook:

   ☐ Bearish   ☐ Neutral   ☐ Bullish

Mid-term Outlook:

   ☐ Bearish   ☐ Neutral   ☐ Bullish

Long-term Outlook:

   ☐ Bearish   ☐ Neutral   ☐ Bullish

TRADE LOG

☐ Bought [Date:_____]	☐ Sold [Date:_____]
Price:	Price:
Quantity:	Quantity:

WHY I LIKE THIS STOCK...

Genius Notes:

STOCK

Company name:

Ticker Symbol:

Industry:

Market Cap: P/E Ratio:

Current Price: Date:

Type:

☐ Value   ☐ Growth   ☐ Dividends

Short-term Outlook:

☐ Bearish   ☐ Neutral   ☐ Bullish

Mid-term Outlook:

☐ Bearish   ☐ Neutral   ☐ Bullish

Long-term Outlook:

☐ Bearish   ☐ Neutral   ☐ Bullish

TRADE LOG

☐ Bought [Date:_____]	☐ Sold [Date:_____]
Price:	Price:
Quantity:	Quantity:

WHY I LIKE THIS STOCK...

Genius Notes:

STOCK

Company name:

Ticker Symbol:

Industry:

Market Cap: P/E Ratio:

Current Price: Date:

Type:

☐ Value   ☐ Growth   ☐ Dividends

Short-term Outlook:

☐ Bearish   ☐ Neutral   ☐ Bullish

Mid-term Outlook:

☐ Bearish   ☐ Neutral   ☐ Bullish

Long-term Outlook:

☐ Bearish   ☐ Neutral   ☐ Bullish

TRADE LOG

☐ Bought [Date:_____]	☐ Sold [Date:_____]
Price:	Price:
Quantity:	Quantity:

WHY I LIKE THIS STOCK...

Genius Notes:

STOCK

Company name:

Ticker Symbol:

Industry:

Market Cap: P/E Ratio:

Current Price: Date:

Type:

    ☐ Value   ☐ Growth   ☐ Dividends

Short-term Outlook:

    ☐ Bearish   ☐ Neutral   ☐ Bullish

Mid-term Outlook:

    ☐ Bearish   ☐ Neutral   ☐ Bullish

Long-term Outlook:

    ☐ Bearish   ☐ Neutral   ☐ Bullish

TRADE LOG

☐ Bought [Date:_____]   ☐ Sold [Date:_____]

Price: Price:

Quantity: Quantity:

WHY I LIKE THIS STOCK...

Genius Notes:

STOCK

Company name:

Ticker Symbol:

Industry:

Market Cap: P/E Ratio:

Current Price: Date:

Type:

☐ Value   ☐ Growth   ☐ Dividends

Short-term Outlook:

☐ Bearish   ☐ Neutral   ☐ Bullish

Mid-term Outlook:

☐ Bearish   ☐ Neutral   ☐ Bullish

Long-term Outlook:

☐ Bearish   ☐ Neutral   ☐ Bullish

TRADE LOG

☐ Bought [Date:_____]	☐ Sold [Date:_____]
Price:	Price:
Quantity:	Quantity:

WHY I LIKE THIS STOCK...

Genius Notes:

STOCK

Company name:

Ticker Symbol:

Industry:

Market Cap: P/E Ratio:

Current Price: Date:

Type:

    ☐ Value   ☐ Growth   ☐ Dividends

Short-term Outlook:

    ☐ Bearish   ☐ Neutral   ☐ Bullish

Mid-term Outlook:

    ☐ Bearish   ☐ Neutral   ☐ Bullish

Long-term Outlook:

    ☐ Bearish   ☐ Neutral   ☐ Bullish

TRADE LOG

☐ Bought [Date:_____]	☐ Sold [Date:_____]
Price:	Price:
Quantity:	Quantity:

WHY I LIKE THIS STOCK...

Genius Notes:

STOCK

Company name:

Ticker Symbol:

Industry:

Market Cap: P/E Ratio:

Current Price: Date:

Type:

☐ Value   ☐ Growth   ☐ Dividends

Short-term Outlook:

☐ Bearish   ☐ Neutral   ☐ Bullish

Mid-term Outlook:

☐ Bearish   ☐ Neutral   ☐ Bullish

Long-term Outlook:

☐ Bearish   ☐ Neutral   ☐ Bullish

TRADE LOG

☐ Bought [Date:_____]	☐ Sold [Date:_____]
Price:	Price:
Quantity:	Quantity:

WHY I LIKE THIS STOCK...

Genius Notes:

STOCK

Company name:

Ticker Symbol:

Industry:

Market Cap: P/E Ratio:

Current Price: Date:

Type:

☐ Value   ☐ Growth   ☐ Dividends

Short-term Outlook:

☐ Bearish   ☐ Neutral   ☐ Bullish

Mid-term Outlook:

☐ Bearish   ☐ Neutral   ☐ Bullish

Long-term Outlook:

☐ Bearish   ☐ Neutral   ☐ Bullish

TRADE LOG

☐ Bought [Date:_____]	☐ Sold [Date:_____]
Price:	Price:
Quantity:	Quantity:

WHY I LIKE THIS STOCK...

Genius Notes:

STOCK

Company name:

Ticker Symbol:

Industry:

Market Cap: P/E Ratio:

Current Price: Date:

Type:

☐ Value   ☐ Growth   ☐ Dividends

Short-term Outlook:

☐ Bearish   ☐ Neutral   ☐ Bullish

Mid-term Outlook:

☐ Bearish   ☐ Neutral   ☐ Bullish

Long-term Outlook:

☐ Bearish   ☐ Neutral   ☐ Bullish

TRADE LOG

☐ Bought [Date:_____]	☐ Sold [Date:_____]
Price:	Price:
Quantity:	Quantity:

WHY I LIKE THIS STOCK...

Genius Notes:

STOCK

Company name:

Ticker Symbol:

Industry:

Market Cap: P/E Ratio:

Current Price: Date:

Type:

☐ Value   ☐ Growth   ☐ Dividends

Short-term Outlook:

☐ Bearish   ☐ Neutral   ☐ Bullish

Mid-term Outlook:

☐ Bearish   ☐ Neutral   ☐ Bullish

Long-term Outlook:

☐ Bearish   ☐ Neutral   ☐ Bullish

TRADE LOG

☐ Bought [Date:_____]	☐ Sold [Date:_____]
Price:	Price:
Quantity:	Quantity:

WHY I LIKE THIS STOCK...

Genius Notes:

STOCK

Company name:

Ticker Symbol:

Industry:

Market Cap: P/E Ratio:

Current Price: Date:

Type:

☐ Value   ☐ Growth   ☐ Dividends

Short-term Outlook:

☐ Bearish   ☐ Neutral   ☐ Bullish

Mid-term Outlook:

☐ Bearish   ☐ Neutral   ☐ Bullish

Long-term Outlook:

☐ Bearish   ☐ Neutral   ☐ Bullish

TRADE LOG

☐ Bought [Date:_____]	☐ Sold [Date:_____]
Price:	Price:
Quantity:	Quantity:

WHY I LIKE THIS STOCK...

Genius Notes:

STOCK

Company name:

Ticker Symbol:

Industry:

Market Cap: P/E Ratio:

Current Price: Date:

Type:

☐ Value ☐ Growth ☐ Dividends

Short-term Outlook:

☐ Bearish ☐ Neutral ☐ Bullish

Mid-term Outlook:

☐ Bearish ☐ Neutral ☐ Bullish

Long-term Outlook:

☐ Bearish ☐ Neutral ☐ Bullish

TRADE LOG

☐ Bought [Date:_____]	☐ Sold [Date:_____]
Price:	Price:
Quantity:	Quantity:

WHY I LIKE THIS STOCK...

Genius Notes:

STOCK

Company name:

Ticker Symbol:

Industry:

Market Cap: P/E Ratio:

Current Price: Date:

Type:
    ☐ Value   ☐ Growth   ☐ Dividends

Short-term Outlook:
    ☐ Bearish   ☐ Neutral   ☐ Bullish

Mid-term Outlook:
    ☐ Bearish   ☐ Neutral   ☐ Bullish

Long-term Outlook:
    ☐ Bearish   ☐ Neutral   ☐ Bullish

TRADE LOG

☐ Bought [Date:_____]   ☐ Sold [Date:_____]

Price: Price:

Quantity: Quantity:

WHY I LIKE THIS STOCK...

Genius Notes:

STOCK

Company name:

Ticker Symbol:

Industry:

Market Cap: P/E Ratio:

Current Price: Date:

Type:
   ☐ Value   ☐ Growth   ☐ Dividends

Short-term Outlook:
   ☐ Bearish   ☐ Neutral   ☐ Bullish

Mid-term Outlook:
   ☐ Bearish   ☐ Neutral   ☐ Bullish

Long-term Outlook:
   ☐ Bearish   ☐ Neutral   ☐ Bullish

TRADE LOG

☐ Bought [Date:_____]   ☐ Sold [Date:_____]

Price: Price:

Quantity: Quantity:

WHY I LIKE THIS STOCK...

Genius Notes:

STOCK

Company name:

Ticker Symbol:

Industry:

Market Cap: P/E Ratio:

Current Price: Date:

Type:

☐ Value   ☐ Growth   ☐ Dividends

Short-term Outlook:

☐ Bearish   ☐ Neutral   ☐ Bullish

Mid-term Outlook:

☐ Bearish   ☐ Neutral   ☐ Bullish

Long-term Outlook:

☐ Bearish   ☐ Neutral   ☐ Bullish

TRADE LOG

☐ Bought [Date:_____]	☐ Sold [Date:_____]
Price:	Price:
Quantity:	Quantity:

WHY I LIKE THIS STOCK...

Genius Notes:

STOCK

Company name:

Ticker Symbol:

Industry:

Market Cap: P/E Ratio:

Current Price: Date:

Type:
    ☐ Value   ☐ Growth   ☐ Dividends

Short-term Outlook:
    ☐ Bearish   ☐ Neutral   ☐ Bullish

Mid-term Outlook:
    ☐ Bearish   ☐ Neutral   ☐ Bullish

Long-term Outlook:
    ☐ Bearish   ☐ Neutral   ☐ Bullish

TRADE LOG

☐ Bought [Date:_____]	☐ Sold [Date:_____]
Price:	Price:
Quantity:	Quantity:

WHY I LIKE THIS STOCK...

Genius Notes:

STOCK

Company name:

Ticker Symbol:

Industry:

Market Cap: P/E Ratio:

Current Price: Date:

Type:

☐ Value   ☐ Growth   ☐ Dividends

Short-term Outlook:

☐ Bearish   ☐ Neutral   ☐ Bullish

Mid-term Outlook:

☐ Bearish   ☐ Neutral   ☐ Bullish

Long-term Outlook:

☐ Bearish   ☐ Neutral   ☐ Bullish

TRADE LOG

☐ Bought [Date:_____]	☐ Sold [Date:_____]
Price:	Price:
Quantity:	Quantity:

WHY I LIKE THIS STOCK...

Genius Notes:

STOCK

Company name:

Ticker Symbol:

Industry:

Market Cap: P/E Ratio:

Current Price: Date:

Type:

   ☐ Value   ☐ Growth   ☐ Dividends

Short-term Outlook:

   ☐ Bearish   ☐ Neutral   ☐ Bullish

Mid-term Outlook:

   ☐ Bearish   ☐ Neutral   ☐ Bullish

Long-term Outlook:

   ☐ Bearish   ☐ Neutral   ☐ Bullish

TRADE LOG

☐ Bought [Date:_____]	☐ Sold [Date:_____]
Price:	Price:
Quantity:	Quantity:

WHY I LIKE THIS STOCK...

Genius Notes:

STOCK

Company name:

Ticker Symbol:

Industry:

Market Cap: P/E Ratio:

Current Price: Date:

Type:

☐ Value   ☐ Growth   ☐ Dividends

Short-term Outlook:

☐ Bearish   ☐ Neutral   ☐ Bullish

Mid-term Outlook:

☐ Bearish   ☐ Neutral   ☐ Bullish

Long-term Outlook:

☐ Bearish   ☐ Neutral   ☐ Bullish

TRADE LOG

☐ Bought [Date:_____]   ☐ Sold [Date:_____]

Price: Price:

Quantity: Quantity:

WHY I LIKE THIS STOCK...

Genius Notes:

STOCK

Company name:

Ticker Symbol:

Industry:

Market Cap: P/E Ratio:

Current Price: Date:

Type:

☐ Value   ☐ Growth   ☐ Dividends

Short-term Outlook:

☐ Bearish   ☐ Neutral   ☐ Bullish

Mid-term Outlook:

☐ Bearish   ☐ Neutral   ☐ Bullish

Long-term Outlook:

☐ Bearish   ☐ Neutral   ☐ Bullish

TRADE LOG

☐ Bought [Date:_____]   ☐ Sold [Date:_____]

Price: Price:

Quantity: Quantity:

WHY I LIKE THIS STOCK...

Genius Notes:

STOCK

Company name:

Ticker Symbol:

Industry:

Market Cap: P/E Ratio:

Current Price: Date:

Type:

☐ Value ☐ Growth ☐ Dividends

Short-term Outlook:

☐ Bearish ☐ Neutral ☐ Bullish

Mid-term Outlook:

☐ Bearish ☐ Neutral ☐ Bullish

Long-term Outlook:

☐ Bearish ☐ Neutral ☐ Bullish

TRADE LOG

☐ Bought [Date:_____]	☐ Sold [Date:_____]
Price:	Price:
Quantity:	Quantity:

WHY I LIKE THIS STOCK...

Genius Notes:

STOCK

Company name:

Ticker Symbol:

Industry:

Market Cap: P/E Ratio:

Current Price: Date:

Type:

☐ Value   ☐ Growth   ☐ Dividends

Short-term Outlook:

☐ Bearish   ☐ Neutral   ☐ Bullish

Mid-term Outlook:

☐ Bearish   ☐ Neutral   ☐ Bullish

Long-term Outlook:

☐ Bearish   ☐ Neutral   ☐ Bullish

TRADE LOG

☐ Bought [Date:_____]	☐ Sold [Date:_____]
Price:	Price:
Quantity:	Quantity:

WHY I LIKE THIS STOCK...

Genius Notes:

STOCK

Company name:

Ticker Symbol:

Industry:

Market Cap: P/E Ratio:

Current Price: Date:

Type:

☐ Value   ☐ Growth   ☐ Dividends

Short-term Outlook:

☐ Bearish   ☐ Neutral   ☐ Bullish

Mid-term Outlook:

☐ Bearish   ☐ Neutral   ☐ Bullish

Long-term Outlook:

☐ Bearish   ☐ Neutral   ☐ Bullish

TRADE LOG

☐ Bought [Date:_____]	☐ Sold [Date:_____]
Price:	Price:
Quantity:	Quantity:

WHY I LIKE THIS STOCK...

Genius Notes:

STOCK

Company name:

Ticker Symbol:

Industry:

Market Cap: P/E Ratio:

Current Price: Date:

Type:

☐ Value   ☐ Growth   ☐ Dividends

Short-term Outlook:

☐ Bearish   ☐ Neutral   ☐ Bullish

Mid-term Outlook:

☐ Bearish   ☐ Neutral   ☐ Bullish

Long-term Outlook:

☐ Bearish   ☐ Neutral   ☐ Bullish

TRADE LOG

☐ Bought [Date:_____]   ☐ Sold [Date:_____]

Price: Price:

Quantity: Quantity:

WHY I LIKE THIS STOCK...

Genius Notes:

STOCK

Company name:

Ticker Symbol:

Industry:

Market Cap: P/E Ratio:

Current Price: Date:

Type:

☐ Value ☐ Growth ☐ Dividends

Short-term Outlook:

☐ Bearish ☐ Neutral ☐ Bullish

Mid-term Outlook:

☐ Bearish ☐ Neutral ☐ Bullish

Long-term Outlook:

☐ Bearish ☐ Neutral ☐ Bullish

TRADE LOG

☐ Bought [Date:_____]	☐ Sold [Date:_____]
Price:	Price:
Quantity:	Quantity:

WHY I LIKE THIS STOCK...

Genius Notes:

STOCK

Company name:

Ticker Symbol:

Industry:

Market Cap: P/E Ratio:

Current Price: Date:

Type:

☐ Value   ☐ Growth   ☐ Dividends

Short-term Outlook:

☐ Bearish   ☐ Neutral   ☐ Bullish

Mid-term Outlook:

☐ Bearish   ☐ Neutral   ☐ Bullish

Long-term Outlook:

☐ Bearish   ☐ Neutral   ☐ Bullish

TRADE LOG

☐ Bought [Date:_____]	☐ Sold [Date:_____]
Price:	Price:
Quantity:	Quantity:

WHY I LIKE THIS STOCK...

Genius Notes:

STOCK

Company name:

Ticker Symbol:

Industry:

Market Cap: P/E Ratio:

Current Price: Date:

Type:

☐ Value   ☐ Growth   ☐ Dividends

Short-term Outlook:

☐ Bearish   ☐ Neutral   ☐ Bullish

Mid-term Outlook:

☐ Bearish   ☐ Neutral   ☐ Bullish

Long-term Outlook:

☐ Bearish   ☐ Neutral   ☐ Bullish

TRADE LOG

☐ Bought [Date:_____]	☐ Sold [Date:_____]
Price:	Price:
Quantity:	Quantity:

WHY I LIKE THIS STOCK...

Genius Notes:

STOCK

Company name:

Ticker Symbol:

Industry:

Market Cap: P/E Ratio:

Current Price: Date:

Type:

   ☐ Value   ☐ Growth   ☐ Dividends

Short-term Outlook:

   ☐ Bearish   ☐ Neutral   ☐ Bullish

Mid-term Outlook:

   ☐ Bearish   ☐ Neutral   ☐ Bullish

Long-term Outlook:

   ☐ Bearish   ☐ Neutral   ☐ Bullish

TRADE LOG

☐ Bought [Date:_____]   ☐ Sold [Date:_____]

Price: Price:

Quantity: Quantity:

WHY I LIKE THIS STOCK...

Genius Notes:

STOCK

Company name:

Ticker Symbol:

Industry:

Market Cap: P/E Ratio:

Current Price: Date:

Type:

☐ Value   ☐ Growth   ☐ Dividends

Short-term Outlook:

☐ Bearish   ☐ Neutral   ☐ Bullish

Mid-term Outlook:

☐ Bearish   ☐ Neutral   ☐ Bullish

Long-term Outlook:

☐ Bearish   ☐ Neutral   ☐ Bullish

TRADE LOG

☐ Bought [Date:_____]   ☐ Sold [Date:_____]

Price: Price:

Quantity: Quantity:

WHY I LIKE THIS STOCK...

Genius Notes:

STOCK

Company name:

Ticker Symbol:

Industry:

Market Cap: P/E Ratio:

Current Price: Date:

Type:

   ☐ Value   ☐ Growth   ☐ Dividends

Short-term Outlook:

   ☐ Bearish   ☐ Neutral   ☐ Bullish

Mid-term Outlook:

   ☐ Bearish   ☐ Neutral   ☐ Bullish

Long-term Outlook:

   ☐ Bearish   ☐ Neutral   ☐ Bullish

TRADE LOG

☐ Bought [Date:_____]	☐ Sold [Date:_____]
Price:	Price:
Quantity:	Quantity:

WHY I LIKE THIS STOCK...

Genius Notes:

STOCK

Company name:

Ticker Symbol:

Industry:

Market Cap: P/E Ratio:

Current Price: Date:

Type:

☐ Value   ☐ Growth   ☐ Dividends

Short-term Outlook:

☐ Bearish   ☐ Neutral   ☐ Bullish

Mid-term Outlook:

☐ Bearish   ☐ Neutral   ☐ Bullish

Long-term Outlook:

☐ Bearish   ☐ Neutral   ☐ Bullish

TRADE LOG

☐ Bought [Date:_____]	☐ Sold [Date:_____]
Price:	Price:
Quantity:	Quantity:

WHY I LIKE THIS STOCK...

Genius Notes:

STOCK

Company name:

Ticker Symbol:

Industry:

Market Cap: P/E Ratio:

Current Price: Date:

Type:

☐ Value   ☐ Growth   ☐ Dividends

Short-term Outlook:

☐ Bearish   ☐ Neutral   ☐ Bullish

Mid-term Outlook:

☐ Bearish   ☐ Neutral   ☐ Bullish

Long-term Outlook:

☐ Bearish   ☐ Neutral   ☐ Bullish

TRADE LOG

☐ Bought [Date:_____]	☐ Sold [Date:_____]
Price:	Price:
Quantity:	Quantity:

WHY I LIKE THIS STOCK...

Genius Notes:

STOCK

Company name:

Ticker Symbol:

Industry:

Market Cap: P/E Ratio:

Current Price: Date:

Type:

 ☐ Value   ☐ Growth   ☐ Dividends

Short-term Outlook:

 ☐ Bearish   ☐ Neutral   ☐ Bullish

Mid-term Outlook:

 ☐ Bearish   ☐ Neutral   ☐ Bullish

Long-term Outlook:

 ☐ Bearish   ☐ Neutral   ☐ Bullish

TRADE LOG

☐ Bought [Date:_____]	☐ Sold [Date:_____]
Price:	Price:
Quantity:	Quantity:

WHY I LIKE THIS STOCK...

Genius Notes:

STOCK

Company name:

Ticker Symbol:

Industry:

Market Cap: P/E Ratio:

Current Price: Date:

Type:

☐ Value   ☐ Growth   ☐ Dividends

Short-term Outlook:

☐ Bearish   ☐ Neutral   ☐ Bullish

Mid-term Outlook:

☐ Bearish   ☐ Neutral   ☐ Bullish

Long-term Outlook:

☐ Bearish   ☐ Neutral   ☐ Bullish

TRADE LOG

☐ Bought [Date:_____]   ☐ Sold [Date:_____]

Price: Price:

Quantity: Quantity:

WHY I LIKE THIS STOCK...

Genius Notes:

STOCK

Company name:

Ticker Symbol:

Industry:

Market Cap: P/E Ratio:

Current Price: Date:

Type:

☐ Value   ☐ Growth   ☐ Dividends

Short-term Outlook:

☐ Bearish   ☐ Neutral   ☐ Bullish

Mid-term Outlook:

☐ Bearish   ☐ Neutral   ☐ Bullish

Long-term Outlook:

☐ Bearish   ☐ Neutral   ☐ Bullish

TRADE LOG

☐ Bought [Date:_____]   ☐ Sold [Date:_____]

Price: Price:

Quantity: Quantity:

WHY I LIKE THIS STOCK...

Genius Notes:

STOCK

Company name:

Ticker Symbol:

Industry:

Market Cap: P/E Ratio:

Current Price: Date:

Type:

☐ Value   ☐ Growth   ☐ Dividends

Short-term Outlook:

☐ Bearish   ☐ Neutral   ☐ Bullish

Mid-term Outlook:

☐ Bearish   ☐ Neutral   ☐ Bullish

Long-term Outlook:

☐ Bearish   ☐ Neutral   ☐ Bullish

TRADE LOG

☐ Bought [Date:_____]	☐ Sold [Date:_____]
Price:	Price:
Quantity:	Quantity:

WHY I LIKE THIS STOCK...

Genius Notes:

STOCK

Company name:

Ticker Symbol:

Industry:

Market Cap: P/E Ratio:

Current Price: Date:

Type:

   ☐ Value   ☐ Growth   ☐ Dividends

Short-term Outlook:

   ☐ Bearish   ☐ Neutral   ☐ Bullish

Mid-term Outlook:

   ☐ Bearish   ☐ Neutral   ☐ Bullish

Long-term Outlook:

   ☐ Bearish   ☐ Neutral   ☐ Bullish

TRADE LOG

☐ Bought [Date:_____]	☐ Sold [Date:_____]
Price:	Price:
Quantity:	Quantity:

WHY I LIKE THIS STOCK...

Genius Notes:

STOCK

Company name:

Ticker Symbol:

Industry:

Market Cap: P/E Ratio:

Current Price: Date:

Type:

☐ Value ☐ Growth ☐ Dividends

Short-term Outlook:

☐ Bearish ☐ Neutral ☐ Bullish

Mid-term Outlook:

☐ Bearish ☐ Neutral ☐ Bullish

Long-term Outlook:

☐ Bearish ☐ Neutral ☐ Bullish

TRADE LOG

☐ Bought [Date:_____]	☐ Sold [Date:_____]
Price:	Price:
Quantity:	Quantity:

WHY I LIKE THIS STOCK...

Genius Notes:

STOCK

Company name:

Ticker Symbol:

Industry:

Market Cap: P/E Ratio:

Current Price: Date:

Type:

☐ Value   ☐ Growth   ☐ Dividends

Short-term Outlook:

☐ Bearish   ☐ Neutral   ☐ Bullish

Mid-term Outlook:

☐ Bearish   ☐ Neutral   ☐ Bullish

Long-term Outlook:

☐ Bearish   ☐ Neutral   ☐ Bullish

TRADE LOG

☐ Bought [Date:_____]	☐ Sold [Date:_____]
Price:	Price:
Quantity:	Quantity:

WHY I LIKE THIS STOCK...

Genius Notes:

STOCK

Company name:

Ticker Symbol:

Industry:

Market Cap: P/E Ratio:

Current Price: Date:

Type:

☐ Value   ☐ Growth   ☐ Dividends

Short-term Outlook:

☐ Bearish   ☐ Neutral   ☐ Bullish

Mid-term Outlook:

☐ Bearish   ☐ Neutral   ☐ Bullish

Long-term Outlook:

☐ Bearish   ☐ Neutral   ☐ Bullish

TRADE LOG

☐ Bought [Date:_____]	☐ Sold [Date:_____]
Price:	Price:
Quantity:	Quantity:

WHY I LIKE THIS STOCK...

Genius Notes:

STOCK

Company name:

Ticker Symbol:

Industry:

Market Cap: P/E Ratio:

Current Price: Date:

Type:

    ☐ Value   ☐ Growth   ☐ Dividends

Short-term Outlook:

    ☐ Bearish   ☐ Neutral   ☐ Bullish

Mid-term Outlook:

    ☐ Bearish   ☐ Neutral   ☐ Bullish

Long-term Outlook:

    ☐ Bearish   ☐ Neutral   ☐ Bullish

TRADE LOG

☐ Bought [Date:_____]   ☐ Sold [Date:_____]

Price: Price:

Quantity: Quantity:

WHY I LIKE THIS STOCK...

Genius Notes:

STOCK

Company name:

Ticker Symbol:

Industry:

Market Cap: P/E Ratio:

Current Price: Date:

Type:

☐ Value   ☐ Growth   ☐ Dividends

Short-term Outlook:

☐ Bearish   ☐ Neutral   ☐ Bullish

Mid-term Outlook:

☐ Bearish   ☐ Neutral   ☐ Bullish

Long-term Outlook:

☐ Bearish   ☐ Neutral   ☐ Bullish

TRADE LOG

☐ Bought [Date:_____]	☐ Sold [Date:_____]
Price:	Price:
Quantity:	Quantity:

WHY I LIKE THIS STOCK...

Genius Notes:

Made in the USA
Monee, IL
12 August 2021

75532558R00069